PETER

- AND THE -

LEMON

MERINGUE

PIE

NINA B. MARINO

PETER
- AND THE -
LEMON MERINGUE PIE

NINA B. MARINO

Published by:

Happiness House Books

(An imprint of The Righteous Pen Publications Group)

www.righteouspenpublications.com

ISBN: 1-940197-71-6
13-Digit: 978-1-940197-71-5

Printed in the United States of America.

DEDICATION

For Peter,
who loved my lemon meringue pie.

Peter was the neighbor boy

Who lived across the way.

He was tall and blonde,

And always loved to play.

His house was down an old dirt road

A vision to behold:

It was long and winding,

With many stories to be told.

You ordered snow, right

THE STORIES TOLD OF ICE AND SNOW,

OF MUD AND DIRT AND WOES;

OF TIRES SPINNING INTO THE GROUND

CRYING TO RELEASE THEIR POSE.

His house was built of stone and rock,
Deep in the woods and trees.
A wonderful place for a neighbor boy
To scratch and skin his knees!

His parents were really great,
As all good neighbors should be.
They were kind, they were caring,
And oh, so sweet to see!

Peter loved his family,

They were all really neat!

His mom, his dad, his sister,

They were all very sweet.

Hɪs ᴅᴀᴅ ᴡᴀꜱ ᴛᴀʟʟ,

Wᴀʏ ᴛᴀʟʟᴇʀ ᴛʜᴀɴ ᴍᴇ!

I ᴡᴏᴜʟᴅ ꜱᴀʏ ʜᴇ ᴡᴀꜱ ᴀʙᴏᴜᴛ ꜱɪx-ꜰᴏᴏᴛ-ᴛʜʀᴇᴇ.

Nᴏ ᴡᴏɴᴅᴇʀ Pᴇᴛᴇʀ ɢʀᴇᴡ ᴛᴏ ʙᴇ

ᴡᴀʏ ᴛᴀʟʟᴇʀ ᴛʜᴀɴ ᴍᴇ!

HIS MOM WAS A CRAFTER,

WORKING HARD ALL-THE-DAY THROUGH!

MAKING JEWELRY AND GIFTS

FOR ME AND FOR YOU.

P ETER HAD ONE SISTER,

SHE COMPLETED HIS FAMILY,

THEY GREW TOGETHER, THEY PLAYED TOGETHER

OH! SO LOVINGLY.

PETER GREW TALL,

HE GREW PROUD.

WITH A KIND, GENTLE SPIRIT

THAT WAS ALWAYS AROUND.

WE HAD AN AGREEMENT,

PETER AND ME.

WHEN HE GOT TALLER THAN ME,

HE WOULD HAVE TO FLEE! (HA, HA!)

PETER WAS GOOD,

SO, YOU COULD SEE.

PETER WAS KIND,

HE HAD RESPECT FOR ALL HUMANITY!

HE LOVED ALL THE ANIMALS,

EVERY SORT AND KIND.

NO MATTER WHAT THE SPECIES,

THEY WERE ALWAYS ON HIS MIND.

He loved the flowers,

He loved the trees.

He loved Mother Nature,

And all her honeybees!

A WONDERFUL NEIGHBOR BOY WAS HE,

HE LOVED THE ANIMALS AND FLOWERS,

SO SWEET.

SWEET AND KIND AS A BOY COULD BE,

AND HE REALLY, REALLY LOVED TO EAT!

HE LOVED ALL FOOD -

COOKIES, CAKES AND PIES.

SPAGHETTI AND MEATBALLS

WERE A FEAST FOR HIS EYES!

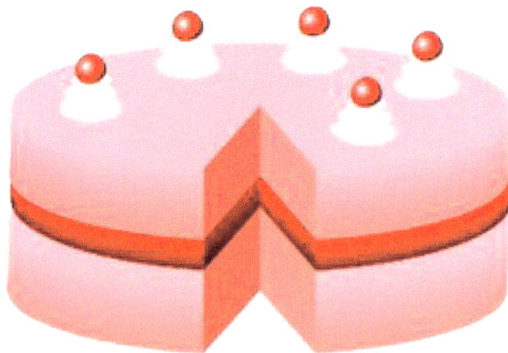

BUT HIS ABSOLUTE FAVORITE

WAS A SIGHT TO BEHOLD:

A LEMON MERINGUE PIE

TOPPED WITH CLOUD-FILLED FOLDS!

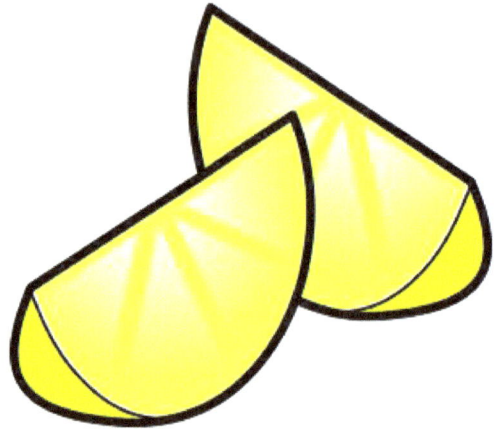

He loved this pie
With its cloud-filled folds.
It was sweet, it was sassy,
It was a sight to behold.

Its clouds were all swirled,

Topped with bronze-colored hue.

The middle was yellow,

Soft and gooey, too.

Its crust was all crunchy,

All golden and brown.

It was a sure bet

How long it would be around.

It was like heaven on earth,
Right there on a plate.
It was absolutely delicious,
And left him feeling great!

He was always so grateful
For that pie that was made
And was filled with a spirit
That could not be decayed.

PETER LOVED IT!

HE LOVED IT SO!

IT WOULD ALWAYS BE A MEMORY,

EVEN AS HE WOULD GROW OLD.

The years flew by,

As they usually do.

Quickly and swiftly,

Peter grew...and grew...and grew!

Today he is a man,

but is still like that boy:

Caring for others,

Bringing knowledge and joy.

The memories are there
Of a time long ago,
When a lemon meringue pie
Was a sight to behold.

A SIGHT OF LOVE AND SHARING,

OF A KINDNESS ONCE BESTOWED

ON A KIND, YOUNG NEIGHBOR BOY,

WITH A STORY NOW BEEN TOLD.

PETER IS A REAL PERSON AND WAS A REAL-TIME NEIGHBOR MANY YEARS AGO. HIS FAMILY AND I WERE CLOSE NEIGHBORS AND FRIENDS FOR SEVERAL YEARS. HE HAD A WONDERFUL, KIND FAMILY WHO GAVE SPECIAL MEANING TO THE WORD AND CONCEPT OF BEING A NEIGHBOR. IT WAS A SPECIAL TREAT TO LIVE CLOSE TO HIS FAMILY AND WATCH PETER GROW UP. WE HAVE MANAGED TO KEEP IN TOUCH OVER THE YEARS. TODAY'S TECHNOLOGY ALLOWS ME TO KEEP IN TOUCH WITH HIM AND CONTINUE BEING HIS NEIGHBOR, EVEN IF IT'S NOW FROM A DISTANCE. IT WAS MY PLEASURE TO WRITE THIS STORY ABOUT HIM.

(NINA B. MARINO, AUTHOR)

ABOUT THE AUTHOR

NINA B. MARINO is a Registered Nurse and Legal Nurse Consultant. She was involved in the nursing profession for over 40 years and in legal nurse consulting for over 20 years. Nina also works and operates in Christian ministry. She was ordained to the office of Prophet in January 2022. She is an original member of Sanctuary International Fellowship Tabernacle (SIFT) in Charlotte, North Carolina, where she serves as an elder.

Nina has loved the written word for a long time, especially reading and sharing books with children. She is the author of four different children's books, including *Gideon - A Yellow Lab: A Love Story*, *Loving Fiona: The Story of a Very Special Dog*, *Peter and the Lemon Meringue Pie*, and *Fruit of the Spirit: God's Code for Living*.

Her work with children has spanned as a mother, grandmother, school nurse, and childhood educator for well over 60 years. She loves crafting, cooking, reading, and working as a Sunday School teacher. In her crafting work, she is a designer for Rose of Sharon Creations. To learn more about Nina, visit:

www.roseofsharoncreations.com.

www.ingramcontent.com/pod-product-compliance
Lightning Source LLC
Chambersburg PA
CBHW060845270326
41933CB00003B/199